To Chuck

Thank you for believing in me! Without your love and support none of this would have been possible.
Love, Ami

To Brandon and Nicholas

This book was written from my heart to yours. The two of you are the most precious gifts that God has ever given me. All I ever wanted to be was a mommy. Thanks for making my dreams come true.
I Love You! Mom

Ami,
I Would like to dedicate my part in this book to you for having confidence in me and believing that I could be an asset to this project, and for having the courage to bring your story that comes from the heart, to other families. I pray that this book will be a blessing to many children as well as to you and your family.
Thank You,
Sherri Shoulders

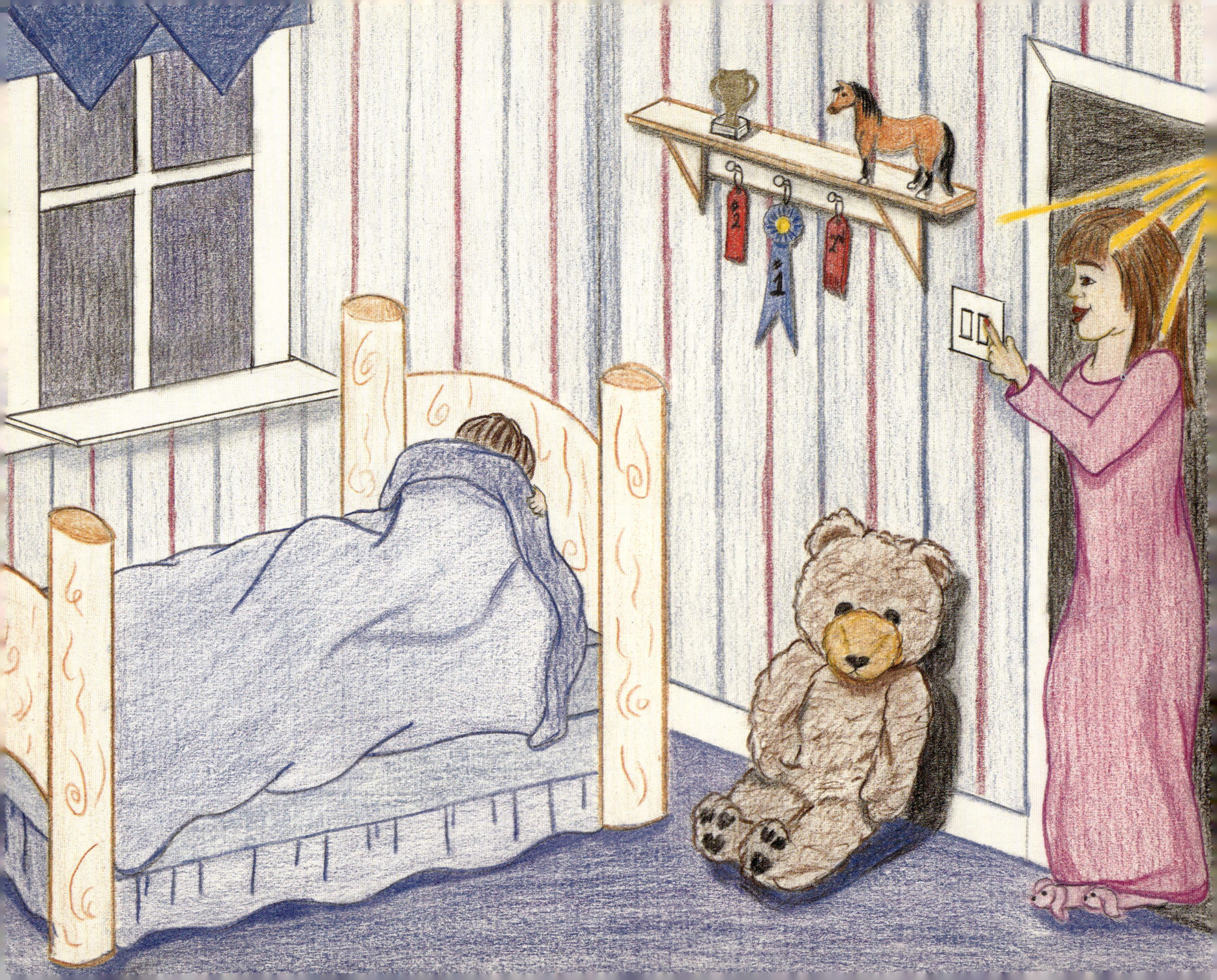

As my mommy reached to turn out the light she said, "Goodnight, sweetheart. Get some rest and I'll see you in the morning."

"Mommy, I'm scared. Please don't leave me in here all alone."

"Brandon, you're not alone. God is with you, remember?"

"How do you know He's here? We can't see Him, touch Him, or anything? I want Him to come down here and lay beside me. Then I won't be scared. God is really tough, isn't He?"

My mom sat down on the bed beside me, and she told me that, "God doesn't have to come down here. He loves you and is already with you."

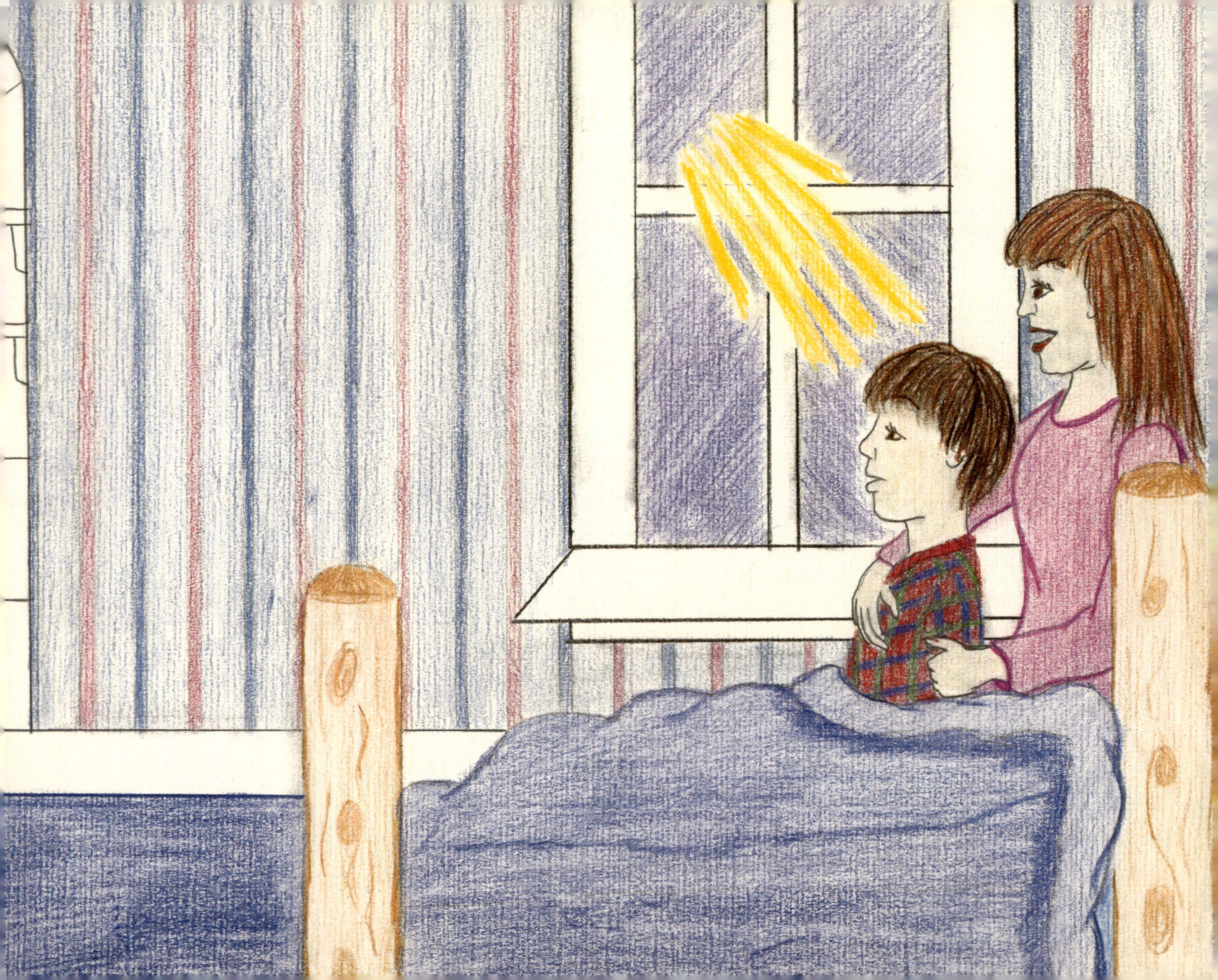

"But how do I know that God loves me?" I asked.

"Because the Bible tells us that He does, and I believe that He is in our hearts," my Mom replied.

"He's in my heart?"

"Yes. Here let me show you. Put your hand over your heart and feel God's love inside of you. If you are really quiet and listen very closely, you'll feel God's love in every beat of your heart and it is like God is saying 'I love you, I love you, I love you, I love you... ... ...'"

"Wow, Mom you're right! I can feel it!"

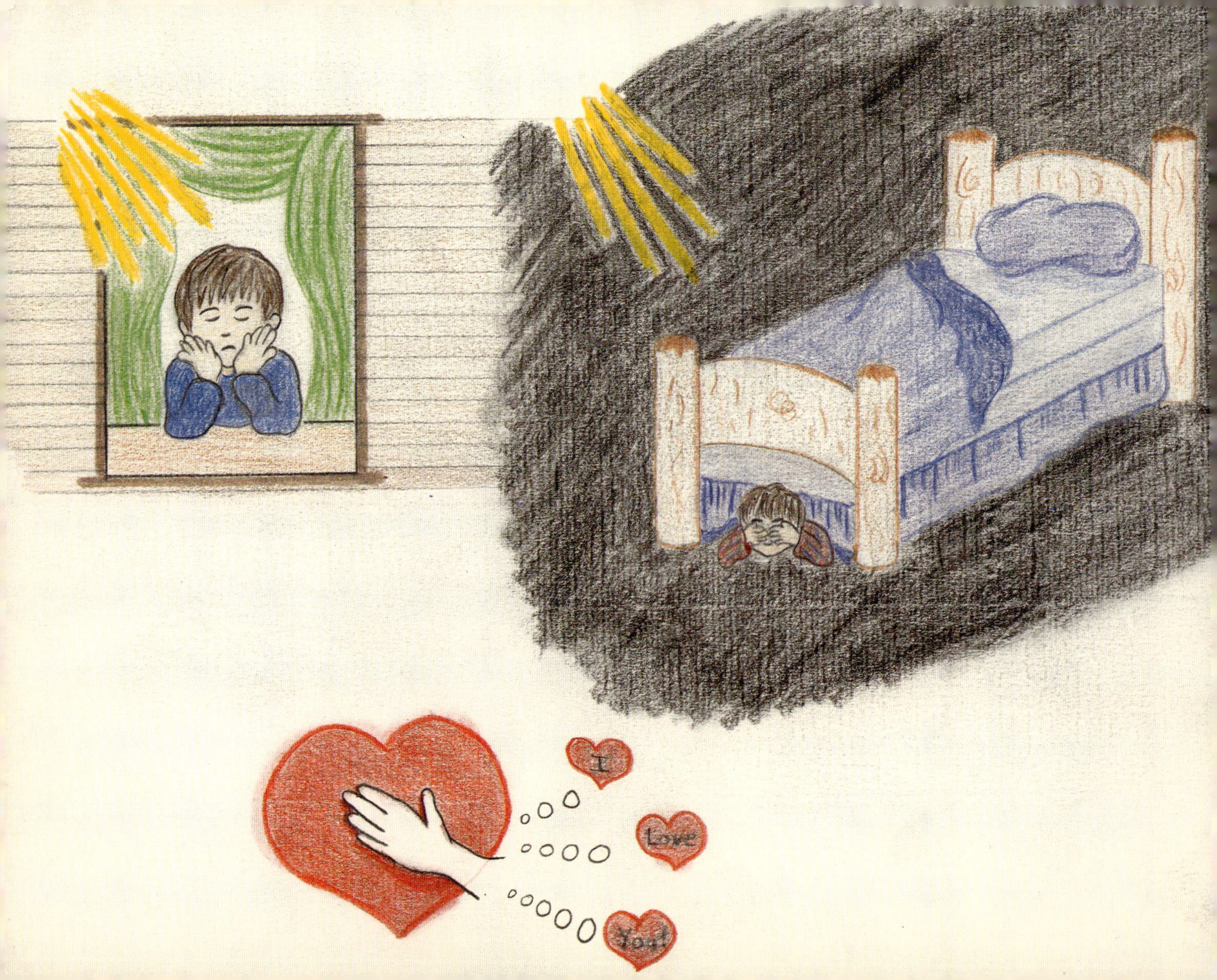
I
Love
You!

Mommy went on, "Whenever you feel lonely, scared, bad, or sad, you can put your hand over your heart and feel God's love and imagine Him saying, 'I love you, I love you, I love you, I love you... ... ...' That will help you remember that He is always with you and He always, always loves you."

Aa Bb Cc Dd Ee Ff Gg
March
1 2 3 4 5
6 7 8 9 10 11 12
13 14 15 16 17 18 19
20 21 22 23 24 25 26
27 28 29 30 31

I thought about what my mommy had said and asked, "You mean no matter where I go or what I do, God is with me, and He loves me even when I'm bad?"

Mommy smiled and said, "Yes honey, no matter where you go or what you do, good or bad, God is with you and He loves you. Although, He wants you to always try to do the right thing, wherever you are and whomever you are with."

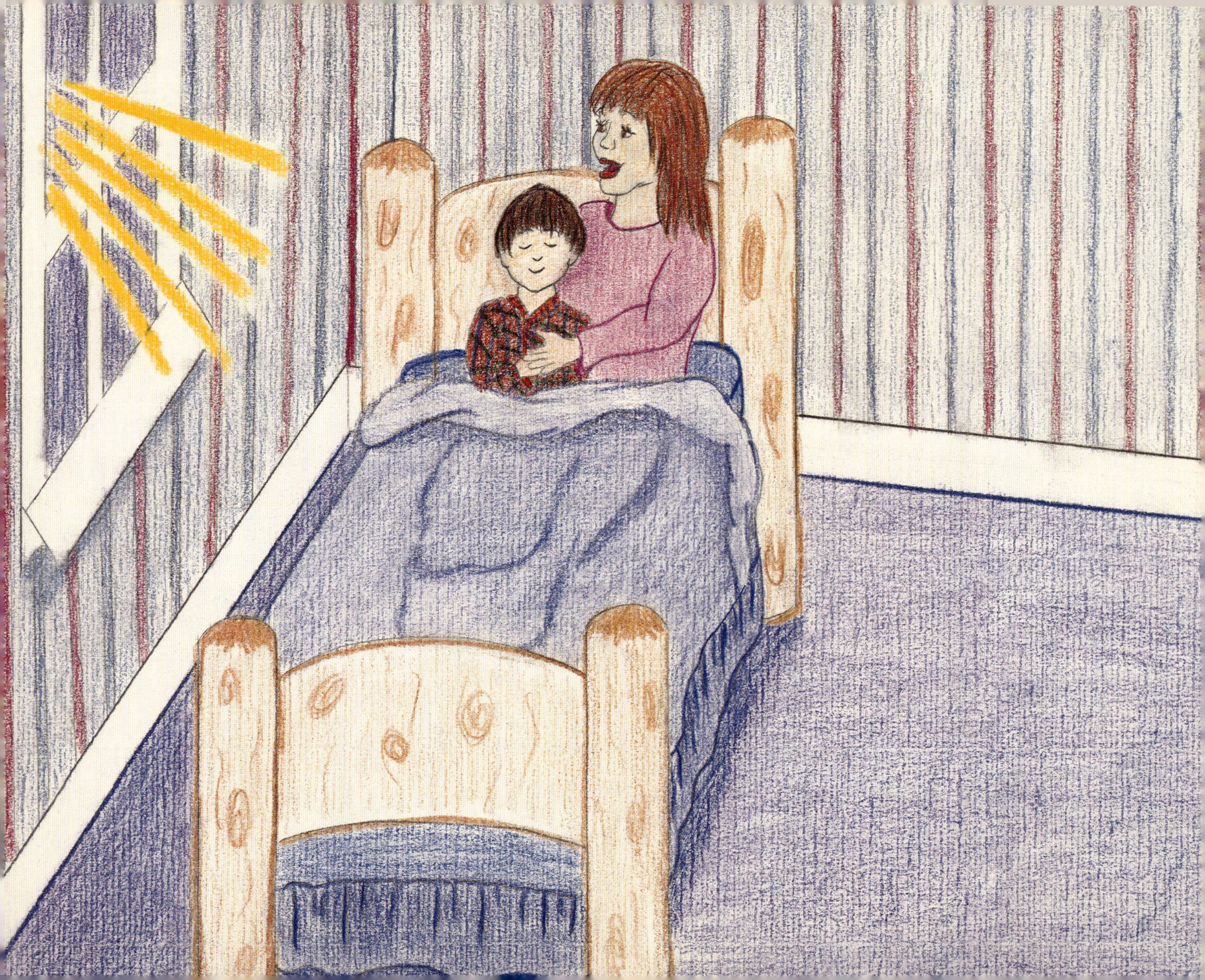

"Mommy, does God love you, too?"

My mommy kissed me goodnight and said, "He sure does. You see God loves everyone. He is in our hearts, if we will just listen to Him. 'I love you, I love you, I love you, I love you, I love you, I love you, … … … … …'"